Best
of
the
West
Biographies

Bill Pickett

Wild West Cowboy

Elaine Landau

Enslow Publishers, Inc.

40 Industrial Road   PO Box 38
Box 398   Aldershot
Berkeley Heights, NJ 07922   Hants GU12 6BP
USA   UK

http://www.enslow.com

Library of Congress Cataloging-in-Publication Data

Landau, Elaine.
     Bill Pickett : wild west cowboy / Elaine Landau.
         p. cm. — (Best of the West biographies)
     Summary: A biography of the black Texan who introduced
bulldogging to rodeos.
     Includes bibliographical references and index.
     ISBN 0-7660-2215-3
     1. Pickett, Bill, ca. 1860-1932—Juvenile literature. 2. African
American cowboys—Biography—Juvenile literature. 3. Rodeos—
United States—History—Juvenile literature. [1. Pickett, Bill, ca.
1860–1932. 2. Cowboys. 3. African Americans—Biography.] I.
Title. II. Series.
GV1833.6.P5L36 2004
796.8'4'092—dc21

                                    2003010332

Printed in the United States of America

10 9 8 7 6 5 4 3 2 1

Contents

Bill Pickett sits on his horse, Spradley. Bill Pickett had found Spradley near death. He stayed with the horse until it was well.

Quite a Cowboy

It was a hot summer day in the late 1880s. Things were winding down at a Texas cattle ranch. A lone cowboy on horseback was bringing in a herd of longhorns. It had been a hard day. The young cowboy was tired and covered with dust. But his work was nearly done. Most of the cows were in the corral.

Then one of the steers bolted. The animal would not enter the corral. Rushing past the other cattle, it broke into a run. Within seconds, the nearly six-hundred-pound longhorn was headed for the range.

The cowboy was out of patience. That steer had been trouble all day. Earlier it would not move with the others. It had started a ruckus that caused the herd to scatter. Now the cowboy and ornery steer were headed for a showdown.

The cowboy knew there was no time to waste. Turning his horse around, he took off after the steer. He had to think fast. When his horse was next to the longhorn, he jumped onto the steer's back. The longhorn tried to throw him off. It bucked and pawed the earth. The steer and the cowboy were in for the fight of their lives.

The cowboy was determined to win. Sliding off the animal, he grabbed its horns. The cowboy tried to wrestle the steer to the ground. It was not easy. The longhorn was both angry and frightened. It snorted and kicked, fighting to break free. The cowboy was in danger. He could be badly hurt or even kicked to death. But he still did not loosen his grip on the animal's horns.

The cowboy knew that he would not be able to hold on much longer. So he did something no other human had done to a steer before. Still holding its horns, the cowboy turned the animal's head toward his. Then he bit the longhorn hard on its upper lip.

The steer was overcome with pain. The animal stopped fighting and its body went limp. The cowboy pushed the steer to the ground. The struggle was over—the cowboy had won.

Bill Pickett was famous for the way he took down steers, but a bulldogger today is no longer allowed to bite the animal's lip.

Cattle drives were long, difficult journeys. Cowboys always had to be on guard for anything that might bring harm to their herds.

Did it really happen that way? No one knows for sure. But that is how people tell the story. It is a story that has been told for more than a hundred years.

Bringing down a cow that way is called bulldogging. Both the method and the man who came up with it later became famous. That man was an African-American cowboy named Bill Pickett.

Most of the cowboys shown in books and movies are white. But that is not how things really were. African-American cowboys played an important role on the American frontier. In Texas alone, they made up about 35 percent of the cowboys. These men drove the cattle herds along dusty trails and worked on ranches. Among the best of them was Bill Pickett.

Pickett was gutsy and tough. He was a proud man who never let any four-legged creature get the best of him. This son of former slaves made quite a name for himself in the Old West. He became one of the best-known African-American cowboys of all time.

African-American Cowboys

Even before the Civil War (1861–1865) there were many African Americans in the West. They had not come there by choice. They were mostly slaves brought west by their white owners. Some of these people had hoped to grow cotton in Texas's rich soil. Others tried their hand at ranching.

Once slavery was over, the ranchers needed cowboys. Some former slaves took these jobs. Black cowboys rode the trails alongside white people. Together, these men drove cattle herds hundreds of miles to the stockyards.

Many African-American cowboys also worked

breaking in horses. Some became rodeo performers as well. African-American cowboys usually enjoyed a good deal of freedom in their work. However, they were still held back because of their race. Only a small number of African Americans ever became ranch managers or foremen.

Bill Picket was not born rich or famous. He came from a poor Texas family. His parents, Thomas and Mary Gilbert Pickett, had been slaves. Like most former slaves, they were freed toward the end of the Civil War. Both were about eleven years old at the time. They eagerly looked forward to a life of freedom.

The couple married when they were in their teens. Before long, they started a family. The Picketts had thirteen children. Bill was the second oldest.

Two dates are often given for his birth. Family members say that Bill was born on December 5, 1870. Yet government records show a date in 1871. Bill went by different names, too. His parents named him William M. Pickett. As a boy, he was usually called Willie. Later on, he was mostly known as Bill.

Bill's parents did their best to care for their growing family. They rented a small plot of land near Austin, Texas. The Picketts lived there and farmed. They grew vegetables to sell at a local market.

Bill's father also did day labor for neighbors and nearby businesses. But there was never enough money. Often, Bill's father could not find work. Even when he did, he was not paid very much.

Bill Pickett's family, like this one shown here, raised crops through hard work in the hot fields.

The family still got by. Everyone did what they could to help. None of the Pickett children were lazy. They worked on the farm as well as did household chores. The children tried to find jobs after school, too.

Bill was a quick learner with a good sense of humor. He learned to read and write at an early age. Although he liked school, he dropped out after the fifth grade. Like most young people from poor families, he had to work. Finishing school was a luxury—one that the Picketts could not afford.

Although he was just a boy, Bill Pickett already knew what he wanted to do. He longed to be a cowboy. Bill had seen cowboys from nearby ranches. He admired their skill in handling cattle and horses. Two of Bill Pickett's older cousins were cowboys. He always looked forward to their visits. Bill loved hearing how they roped steers and protected cattle from buffalo stampedes.

Bill also watched other cowboys from nearby ranches. He especially liked seeing them

Buffalo, the largest American animal, used to roam the prairies in large numbers. Today, however, most of them live on wildlife preserves.

work with wild horses. Bill studied their moves. He tried to learn from their mistakes. The boy wanted to know everything about ranch work.

People say that was how he got the idea for bulldogging. Bill saw that ranchers used bulldogs to bring in stray cattle. These dogs were trained to grab hold of a steer's lip with their teeth. The pain made the steer stop struggling. Once the animal was quiet, a cowboy would rope it. Bill thought that if a dog

could control a steer this way, so could he. He
tried it on a few strays and was not surprised
when it worked.

Before long, Bill Pickett had a chance to
show off his new skill. One afternoon he saw a

**Each ranch had a different brand that identified its
cattle. A brand was made by applying hot iron to
the animal to burn its skin and leave a scar.**

group of cowboys branding some calves. They were having a hard time because the frightened animals would not hold still. Bill offered to help. He claimed that he could quiet the calves.

The cowboys doubted it, but they decided to let him try. A roped and tied calf was already on the ground. Bill bit into its lip. The calf stopped fighting. Young Bill Pickett did not let go of the animal's lip until the cowboys finished branding it.

It is very difficult to tame a wild horse.

The cowboys were glad that Bill had been there that day.

After that, Bill could not wait to become a cowboy. At fifteen, he began working on ranches. He learned how to rope steers and tame wild horses. Bill Pickett worked hard. Before long, he could do everything a cowboy did. He was as good as any man in the region.

A Rodeo Star

Being a cowboy was not easy. Bill Pickett often worked over eighty hours a week. That is more than twice as long as most people work today. A cowboy's job was not always pleasant, either. At times, Pickett was outdoors for hours under the blistering sun. Cowboys worked through heavy rainstorms, as well.

Even though Pickett was often tired, he still practiced his cowboy skills. This came in handy. On Sundays, he sometimes entered bronco-riding contests. At these contests, cowboys rode wild, unbroken horses. Each man tried to stay on his horse as long as possible. These contests could be risky. Cowboys thrown from their horses sometimes broke bones. Many

were kicked by the animals, too. But Bill Pickett was willing to take his chances.

In 1888, the Picketts moved to Taylor, Texas. People there had already heard about Pickett's bulldogging skills. That year, Pickett performed in Taylor's town fair. He was the crowd's favorite.

To win a bronco riding contest, the rider must stay on a bucking horse for eight seconds.

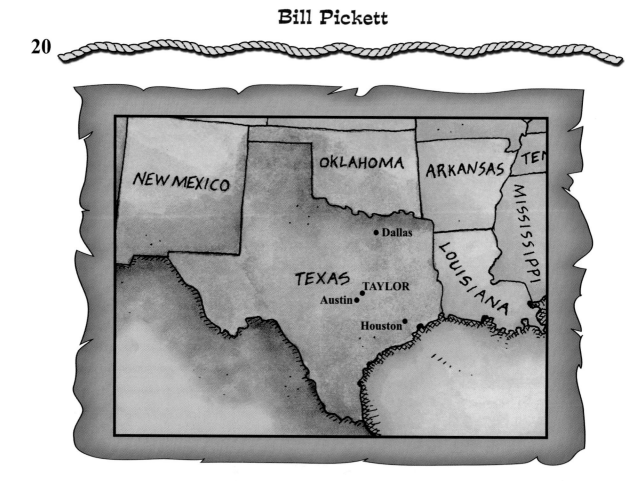

Bill Pickett raised his family in Taylor, Texas.

Bill Pickett came to think of Taylor, Texas as his hometown. He built a life for himself there. Pickett made many friends in Taylor. He also fell in love with a young woman named Maggie Turner. Bill Pickett married Maggie Turner in December 1890.

Bill Pickett had come from a large family.

Now he and Maggie started one of their own. Through the years, they had nine children. There were seven girls and two boys. The couple had high hopes for all their children. However, both their sons died when they were just infants.

During the 1890s, Pickett worked harder than ever. He was always trying to find better ways to support his growing family. At one point, Pickett and his brothers started

In the 1890s, wild horses ran free across the plains of the Southwest. Taming wild horses was important to ranch life.

their own business. It was called Pickett Brothers Bronco Busters and Rough Riders. The brothers tamed wild horses. This was a useful service for local ranchers. Their advertisements stated, "Catching and taming wild cattle a specialty." Bill Pickett was the family's expert at that.

At the same time, Pickett also became active in the community. He had regularly attended church services as a child. Now he and Maggie took their own children to a Baptist church. Pickett later became a church deacon. He sometimes taught Sunday school in his home, too.

Bill Pickett liked his life in Taylor, but he needed to make more money. Pickett was sure that people would pay to see him bulldogging steers. He decided to tour with a rodeo.

A rodeo was the perfect place for Bill Pickett. In these action-packed shows, cowboys showed off their riding and roping skills. Rodeos always included a number of events. Among these were bronco riding, bull riding,

"Spurring" is what the rider does to make the horse buck. He kicks the side of the horse with his boots, which have spurs on the heels.

calf roping, steer roping, and barrel racing. Before Bill Pickett arrived, no rodeo cowboy had ever thrown a full-grown steer to the ground. But Pickett would make bulldogging, or steer wrestling, an exciting rodeo event.

In 1900, Pickett began touring with some small rodeos. These played in cities throughout Texas. It was not long before he was doing shows in other states, as well. The crowds admired his bravery in handling steers. Pickett enjoyed their applause.

However, Bill Pickett's career really soared after he met the Miller brothers. The Millers owned a 100,000-acre ranch in Oklahoma. It was called The 101. They also owned a fabulous traveling Wild West show. Their Wild West show had many rodeo acts. In time, more than ninety cowboys and cowgirls took part in it. The show traveled with over three hundred animals, too.

Bill Pickett joined The 101 Ranch Wild West Show in 1907. He toured with the show several months a year. The rest of the time he worked on the ranch. His family moved there with him. They stayed at the ranch while Pickett was on the road.

Bill Pickett proved to be an extremely popular performer. Known by such nicknames as "The Dusky Demon" and "The Bull Dogger," he drew in large crowds. His way of bringing down steers became known as his "bite-'em" style. The rodeo program described Pickett's act this way: "Throwing Steers by the Nose With His Teeth."

Bill Pickett soon became a rodeo star.

Although their job is not as exciting as a rodeo star, cowboys have the important task of keeping the herd together.

Audiences cheered when he rode out on Spradley, his favorite horse. Pickett often left the crowds breathless. Everyone knew that he could be hurt while in the ring. Although Pickett was strong, he was not an especially large man. He stood 5'7" and only weighed 145 pounds. The animals he took on were much heavier. Many of the steers weighed over 1,000 pounds. Yet Bill Pickett never showed any fear.

This was true even when mishaps occurred. Once as Pickett was toppling a steer, the animal unexpectedly landed on top of him. The audience anxiously waited to see if Pickett was all right. His bones could have been crushed. He also could have been gorged or cut by the animal's sharp horns.

But through it all, Bill Pickett remained calm and in control. Within seconds, he got the steer to roll off him. Then he stood up and waved to the audience. Pickett was hurt but he was too much of a showman to show it. Thunderous applause filled the arena. People left that night talking about the brave African-American cowboy. They thought that Bill Pickett was the best part of the show.

Longhorn steers often appear in rodeos. The rodeo star will wrestle the steer to the ground and hold it there. This painting, called "Texas Longhorns," was done by Olaf C. Seltzer.

4 Living Dangerously

Before long, Bill Pickett became quite well known. His bulldogging act was always exciting. Sometimes, though, things got a little too exciting. That happened once during a show at Madison Square Garden in New York City.

At the time, Pickett was working with a man named Will Rogers. Will Rogers would later become a famous entertainer known for his humor. But this was just the start of Rogers's career. That evening, he was working as Bill Pickett's hazer.

A hazer is a man who helps the rodeo performer. As the hazer, Rogers would ride alongside the steer. That forced the animal to run in a straight line. Bill Pickett rode on the other side of the steer. At the right moment, Pickett would jump off his horse and onto the steer's back.

But that night, things did not go as planned. The steer came out of the arena's chute at an unusually fast pace. It headed straight for the fence separating the performers from the audience. Within seconds, the steer jumped the fence and charged at the crowd.

Panic broke out. People screamed and ran in all directions. They pushed one another and fell in the aisles.

The steer had reached the third balcony level in no time. No one was sure what would happen next.

The always-funny Will Rogers had his own show, the Will Rogers Follies, and starred in over seventy movies.

But Bill Pickett and Will Rogers were not about to wait and see.

The pair rode into the stands. Pickett bulldogged the steer and Rogers roped it. Then they safely brought the animal back to the performance area. The crowd was amazed by the men's daring. The rest of the New York City shows quickly sold out.

Another scary incident took place in 1908 when the 101 Ranch Wild West Show played in Mexico City, Mexico. At the time, most Mexicans were not great rodeo fans. They preferred the sport of bullfighting. However, one of the Miller brothers had bragged about Bill Pickett. He claimed that Pickett was better than any Mexican bullfighter. Miller bet 5,000 pesos (Mexican dollars) that Bill Pickett could bulldog a Mexican fighting bull.

Miller had also said that Pickett would hold on to the bull for a full five minutes. That would make things extremely dangerous for Pickett. Nevertheless, he agreed to do it. He did not want Miller to lose the bet.

The sport of bullfighting has been popular in Spain and Mexico since the 1700s.

Things were tense at show time as Pickett rode into the ring. He slowly neared the bull on his horse, Spradley. But within seconds, the angry bull charged at the horse's rear. It gorged Spradley's hindquarters with its sharp horns. The bleeding horse had to be taken from the ring. Now Bill Pickett faced the bull alone.

Pickett managed to grasp its horns. But the fierce animal tossed Pickett about like a stuffed toy. The thousands of Mexican people in the audience were not rooting for Bill Pickett. They felt that Miller had insulted them when he insulted bullfighting. Now they were ready to see the famous American bulldogger die in the ring. The arena owner had even brought in a black coffin and paraded it around the bull ring. Everyone, including Pickett, knew who it was supposed to be for.

Bill Pickett held on to the bull's horns with his bare hands. Meanwhile, the audience booed him and called him names. They threw bottles, bricks, and stones at Pickett from the stands. Bill Pickett was hit. Three of his ribs were broken. He was also bleeding from several cuts.

Through it all, Bill Pickett clung to that bull. Those five minutes seemed like an hour. But even when the five

Many rodeo shows and bull fights are performed in bull rings, like this one in Pamplona, Spain.

minutes were up, the timekeeper did not ring the bell. The Mexican timekeeper sided with the angry crowd. After six minutes, the 101 Show crew came to Bill's rescue. Bursting into the bull ring, they speedily roped the bull.

Now the crowd was angrier than ever. It looked like a riot might break out. Bill Pickett and the 101 Show crew were in danger. The bull had not killed Pickett, but it looked like the audience might. The President of Mexico, Porfirio Díaz, had to send in soldiers to calm things down. They took the Americans safely to their hotel.

Porfirio Díaz was President of Mexico twice, from 1877–1880, and again from 1884–1911.

Pickett was injured, but both he and Spradley survived. Miller won the bet and collected the money. From then on, he bragged about Bill Pickett even more.

5

The Later Years

Bill Pickett nearly lost his life in Mexico City. But that did not keep him home long. After he got over his wounds, he was back touring. The 101 Ranch Wild West Show played in twenty-two states and in Canada. Pickett also performed in South America with another Wild West show.

Touring was not always easy for Bill Pickett. At times, he had to deal with prejudice against African Americans. In some areas, African-American performers were not welcome. Several Wild West shows with which he toured were not allowed to open if Pickett performed. Therefore, he had to sit out these shows. Nevertheless, thousands of people still had a chance to admire Pickett's bravery and skill. In many ways, his talent helped pave the way for other African-American performers.

In 1914, the 101 Ranch Wild West Show went to London, England. There, Pickett performed before King George V and Queen Mary. The rulers thoroughly enjoyed the show. The 101 Ranch Wild West Show was supposed to tour other European countries, as well.

But that never happened. World War I, a war involving a number of countries, broke out in Europe. The 101 Ranch Wild West Show performers headed home. But it was as if trouble

King George V and Queen Mary were fans of the 101 Ranch Wild West Show.

followed them. In 1917, the United States entered the war, as well.

By then, Pickett was too old to go into the army. So, for a while, he worked as a cowboy. He also starred in several small rodeos. He still worked with steers, but no longer bit them. Animal rights supporters felt that it was cruel and put a stop to it. Now Pickett held on to the steer's horns, twisting its head as he wrestled it to the ground.

Rodeos were not Pickett's only brush with show business. He also appeared in a few movies. He was the first black cowboy to appear in motion pictures.

Pickett's wife, Maggie, liked having her husband close by. When he was on tour, she had felt that she

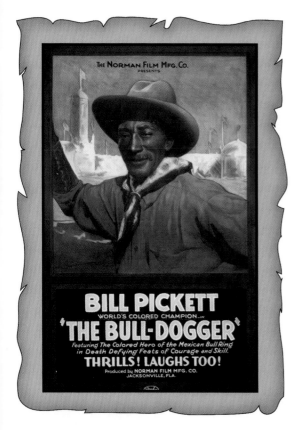

THE NORMAN FILM MFG. CO.
PRESENTS

BILL PICKETT
WORLD'S COLORED CHAMPION...IN
'THE BULL-DOGGER'
Featuring The Colored Hero of the Mexican Bull Ring
in Death Defying Feats of Courage and Skill.
THRILLS! LAUGHS TOO!
Produced by NORMAN FILM MFG. CO.
JACKSONVILLE, FLA.

Bill Pickett's movie, *The Bull-Dogger*, was released in 1921.

never saw enough of him. But as it turned out, there was too little time left for the couple. In 1929, Maggie died. Some said that Bill Pickett was never the same after that.

Things did not go well for the Miller brothers, either. As time passed, their show had not done well. By 1931, they were forced to sell out. Bill Pickett was there near the end. He had been living in a small house on the ranch.

African-American cowboys have their place in Wild West history.

One morning in March 1932, he went to the corral. He wanted to separate the Millers's horses from those belonging to the new owners. There was a terrible accident. Bill Pickett was knocked off a horse. While on the ground, the scared animal kicked him in the head. Although Pickett was bleeding badly, he managed to get up. But he passed out when he tried to walk.

Pickett was taken to the hospital. For the next two weeks, he remained in a coma. There was nothing the doctors could do for him. Bill Pickett died on April 2, 1932. The much-admired rodeo cowboy was buried on a hill overlooking the 101 Ranch. Over two hundred people attended his funeral.

By then, his old friend Will Rogers had his own radio show. He used it to help everyone remember how fine a man Bill Pickett had been. As Will Rogers put it: "Bill Pickett never had an enemy. Even the steers wouldn't hurt old Bill."

6

A Great Performer, a Special Man

Bill Pickett has not been forgotten. He has a special place in rodeo cowboy history. He is remembered for inventing the popular rodeo sport of bulldogging. Before Bill Pickett, no one had wrestled steers in rodeos. Although performers no longer bite the steers today, steer wrestling remains a popular rodeo event.

Bill Pickett has often been honored since his death. In 1971, he became the first African American ever accepted into the National Rodeo Cowboy Hall of Fame in Oklahoma City, Oklahoma. He was also admitted to the Prorodeo Hall of Fame and Museum of the American Cowboy at Colorado Springs, Colorado.

Texas has also taken steps to remember Bill Pickett. A bronze statue of him is on display at

Bulldogging competitions are still held today. This cowboy is wrestling a steer in the Bill Pickett Invitational Rodeo, a modern-day contest.

the North Fort Worth Historical Society. In his hometown of Taylor, Texas, a plaque in a park across from City Hall honors Pickett. It describes his many achievements. There have also been Bill Pickett parades.

In March 1994, Bill Pickett was honored nationally. His picture was put on a U.S. postage stamp. The stamp was part of a series called Legends of the West. People were excited about the stamp but then there was a mix up. The picture on the stamp turned out not to be of Bill. Instead, it was a picture of his younger brother, Ben! The stamps were soon redone with the new ones honoring the real Bill Pickett.

There is also a Bill Pickett Invitational Rodeo. This is the nation's only touring African-American rodeo. The money from the rodeo goes to the Bill Pickett Memorial Scholarship Fund. The fund is used to help students with their education.

Bill Pickett is easy to admire. He worked hard to overcome the odds. He started out poor but became an internationally famous rodeo performer. Through his talent and example, he helped break down racial barriers, as well. As 101 Ranch owner, Zack Miller, said of him: "Bill Pickett was the greatest sweat-and-dirt cowhand that ever lived—bar none."

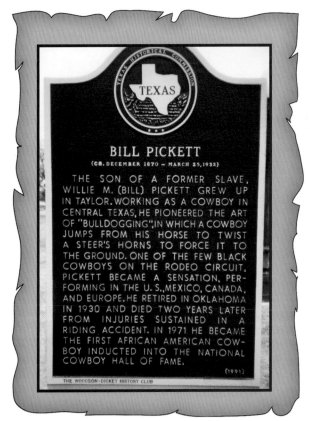

This plaque honors Bill Pickett in his hometown of Taylor, Texas, which is just north of the state capital, Austin.

Timeline

1870 or 1871—Bill Pickett is born on December 5.

1888—The Picketts move to Taylor, Texas.

1890—Bill Pickett marries Maggie Turner.

1890s—Bill Pickett and his brothers start their own business, Pickett Brothers Bronco Busters and Rough Riders.

1900—Pickett begins touring with small rodeos.

1907—Pickett joins the 101 Ranch Wild West Show.

1908—The 101 Ranch Wild West Show performs in Mexico City, Mexico.

1914—The 101 Ranch Wild West Show puts on a show for King George V and Queen Mary in London, England.

1917—The United States enters World War I; Pickett returns to ranch life.

1929—Bill Pickett's wife, Maggie, dies.

1931—The Miller brothers sell the 101 Ranch Wild West Show.

1932—Bill Pickett dies on April 2.

1971—Bill Pickett becomes the first African American ever accepted into the National Rodeo Cowboy Hall of Fame in Oklahoma City, Oklahoma.

1994—Bill Pickett is honored on a United States postage stamp as part of a series called Legends of the West.

Words to Know

arena—A large space where sports are played.

barrel racing—A rodeo event in which a horse and rider race in a zigzag pattern.

branding—Burning a mark onto an animal's skin to show ownership.

bronco—A type of wild horse.

coma—A deep, sleep-like state from which it is hard to wake up.

corral—A fenced holding area for cattle.

deacon—A person who helps the minister of a church.

hazer—A rodeo performer who runs alongside a steer, forcing it to run in a straight line.

herd—A large group of animals.

injured—Wounded or harmed.

longhorn—A breed of cattle that has long horns.

pesos—A unit of money used in Mexico.

prejudice—Dislike of another race or religion based on an unfair opinion.

ruckus—An uproar or disturbance.

stampede—A group of animals making a sudden rush in one direction.

steers—Young male cattle.

stray—To wander about; leaving the herd or group.

tour—The process of traveling from place to place to perform.

Reading About Bill Pickett

Alter, Judy. *Rodeos: The Greatest Show On Dirt*. Danbury, Conn: Franklin Watts, 1996.

Crum, Robert. *Let's Rodeo! Young Buckaroos and the World's Wildest Sport*. New York: Simon & Schuster, 1996.

DeAngelis, Gina. *The Black Cowboys*. Broomall, Penn: Chelsea House Publishing, 1997.

Lester, Julius. *Black Cowboy, Wild Horses; A True Story*. New York: Dial Books, 1998.

McLeese, Tex. *Bronc and Bareback Riding: Rodeo*. Vero Beach, FL: Rourke, 2001.

Pinkney, Andrea Davis. *Bill Pickett: Rodeo-Ridin' Cowboy*. San Diego, Calif.: Harcourt Brace & Co., 1996.

Schlissel, Lillian. *Black Frontiers: A History of African American Heroes in the Old West*. New York: Simon & Schuster, 1995.

Sherman, Josepha. *Ropers and Riders*. Chicago, Ill.: Heinemann Library, 2000.

Sherman, Josepha. *Steer Wrestling*. Chicago, Ill.: Heinemann Library, 2000.

Internet Addresses

The Bill Pickett Invitational Rodeo

Visit the Web site of the rodeo that honors Bill Pickett. Learn about different rodeo events.

<www.billpickettrodeo.com>

The Federation of Black Cowboys

This Web site has photos of African-American cowboys. Learn about African-American cowboys from both the past and present.

<www.federationofblackcowboys.com>

National Cowboy and Western Heritage Museum

Do not miss this great cowboy Web site! The children's interactive section has authentic cowboy games, songs, exhibits, recipes, and online tours.

<www.nationalcowboymuseum.org>

Index

DEMCO